BALTIMORE

AND ITS

STREETCARS

*— a pictorial review
of the postwar years*

by Herbert H. Harwood, Jr.

QUADRANT PRESS, Inc.
19 West 44th Street
New York, N. Y. 10036
☎ (212) 819-0822

ISBN 0-915276-44-5

INTRODUCTION

VIRTUALLY EVERY large city had its streetcar era, each one usually with its own distinct personality. But Baltimore's seemed to be a summary of them all: whatever features other trolley systems had, they were likely to be found somewhere in Baltimore too. Perhaps that's not surprising, since Baltimore always had an unsettled personality. It was partly Old South, partly nineteenth century New England mill town, partly midwestern industrial city, partly cosmopolitan international port, partly office and regional financial center, and partly its own peculiar blend of big city and small town atmospheres.

Whatever the reason, Baltimore's urban transportation system in the first half of this century had diversity and charm almost unequalled elsewhere. Its trolleys lurched through a labyrinth of complex downtown trackwork and along single-track rural jerkwater lines; they threaded through steel mills and shipyards; they rolled past woods, inlets, ponds, amusement park roller coasters and—of course— endless row houses ranging in age from the 1700s to the 1930s. There were the latest PCC cars and turn-of-the-century Brills, which were among the oldest streetcars operating anywhere.

And as a basically conservative, somewhat dowdy city (40 years ago, at least), Baltimore seemed to cling to a streetcar system which in many ways was already archaic. Indeed, it took two "foreign" elements to shake the system into the mid-twentieth century—a traffic commissioner imported from Denver and transfer of the transit company control to Chicago. The changes that followed were undoubtedly inevitable, but much was lost in the process.

This book's purpose is to communicate the diversity and atmosphere of Baltimore's streetcar era as it was in its best-remembered days, and at the same time show something of what the "streetcar city" itself looked like. Thus this is neither a history nor a dissertation on equipment. Already, Baltimore is well covered in those areas. For general history, there is Michael R. Farrell's *Who Made All Our Streetcars Go?* For those interested in the details of the trolleys themselves, two complementary books cover the full range: *Early Electric Cars of Baltimore* by Harold E. Cox and *Baltimore Streetcars 1905-1963* by Bernard J. Sachs, George F. Nixon and Harold E. Cox. All of these may be obtained through the Baltimore Streetcar Museum. Also available from the museum on special order is Kenneth Morse's unpublished monograph "Baltimore Streetcar Routes", a detailed analysis of each car line from birth to death.

In compiling this book, the author quickly discovered that in the 1940s and early 1950s, the enthusiast-photographer with a "scenic sense" was a rare bird. Happily he found several who not only had that sense, but were generous and helpful besides. Most notable were Edward S. Miller of Pittston, Pennsylvania and George J. Voith of Baltimore. Without them, documentation of Baltimore's streetcar era would be far poorer. Equally helpful were Robert S. Crockett, Robert W. Janssen, Fred W. Schneider III, Robert M. Vogel and J. William Vigrass. David B. Ditman read the messy manuscripts and corrected errors in both fact and English. My own debt to them all is extreme; more important, anyone interested in Baltimore's history owes them much.

HERBERT H. HARWOOD, Jr.
Baltimore, Maryland

G. J. Voith

Baltimore's downtown scenery was very different in 1946 as a #6 car for Fairfield rumbled south on Light Street by the McCormick building. Old Bay Line steamboats for Norfolk loaded at the right and the Baltimore Trust tower at the left rear was the major landmark. Now even the names have changed: the Baltimore Trust is the Maryland National Bank, and the building is almost lost in a sea of new high-rise boxes. The "Basin" to the right is now the Inner Harbor, the motley buildings bordering it having been replaced by the sanitized Harborplace, and armies of tourists now populate what was a seedy backwash of the city.

FRONT COVER:
Ancient but impressive, the "red rocket" trains were rolling Baltimore landmarks. Headed by 5181, this pair rumbles past the city's center, Baltimore and Charles Streets, during a Labor Day fan excursion in 1948. Directly to the left is B&O's general office building; to the rear is the locally-revered O'Neill's department store, now replaced by the One Charles Center building.
Color photograph — G. J. Voith.

INSIDE FRONT COVER:
A canopy of trolley wires overhung Fayette and Holliday Streets in September of 1946. Beneath those wires ran the rails of a unique streetcar system. Seen here is one of Baltimore's unusual two-section articulateds picking its way across the switchwork. — *H. H. Harwood, Jr.*

TITLE PAGE:
A wet snow pelts a PCC streamliner running on one of Baltimore's last two car lines as it begins its run at Walbrook Junction. The date is February 15, 1958. By the next morning, the snow was 15 inches deep, virtually paralyzing this semi-southern city. — *F. W. Schneider III.*

CONTENTS

LOOKING BACK

DEPENDING ON how you define it, Baltimore's streetcar era lasted between 73 and 104 years before the last trolley ran in 1963. But Baltimoreans who remember and rode the cars usually think of them as they were in the 1940s, the last decade that they dominated the city's public transportation. This book illustrates that period. Before looking at the pictures, however, we should stop to take a snapshot of the city itself and its streetcar system as it was in one of those last "typical" years—say, 1945.

This was the Indian summer of the Baltimore trolley. World War II had brought back a surge of riders, many of which soon would be driving cars again. A large fleet of fine streamlined PCC cars recently had been delivered and, despite some Depression-era line cutbacks, the system still was large, varied and busy. But winter came quickly afterwards. By the late 1950s, only two trolley lines would be left, motheaten remnants hanging on mostly because the company couldn't afford to buy buses to replace them. In early November 1963, these too finally died and their tracks quickly vanished under asphalt. Today it takes some looking to find physical traces of the transportation system which had built, nourished and expanded the city. Memories hold some images of the cars and lines, but these too are increasingly indistinct.

So let's go back briefly to the way things were in 1945, at the end of the war and the beginning of the end for the streetcar.

Looking at Baltimore today, it is often difficult even to picture the environment in which trolleys ran, much less the system itself. In many ways the Baltimore of 1945 was a wholly different city: different physically, socially, philosophically and economically. Most obvious was its outward appearance. Among other things there was nothing resembling an expressway—no Beltway, no Jones Falls Expressway, no Baltimore-Washington Parkway, no Harbor Tunnel. Instead the autos and trucks, including all intercity traffic, fought their way through city streets. And those streets were mostly two-way, often occupied by double car tracks, and congested—not only by motor and streetcar traffic, but by the multitude of horse-drawn carts of the "street Arabs" or "hucksters" which were still determinedly part of Baltimore's tradition. Many streets still had brick or stone block

paving. Synchronized traffic lights were almost nonexistent and parking regulations were considerably more casual than now. In all, local driving was a creeping, confused and often bumpy ordeal.

To be sure, a few bold efforts already had been made to speed the ever-growing flow of motor traffic through Baltimore's archaic street layout. The Orleans Street viaduct had been open for nine years, and the Howard Street extension and bridge, which created a much-needed new north-south route, was five years old. Significantly, neither of these improvements included trolley tracks. In fact, two car lines had been abandoned and several others rerouted so as not to hinder motor traffic on the new corridors.

Like most cities before the expressway era, Baltimore was basically more compact. People clustered closer to the city's center and many more worked downtown. The downtown they traveled to, usually by trolley, was a different downtown, too. No Charles Center, of course—nor Civic Center, nor Convention Center nor Inner Harbor development. In their place was a haphazard jumble of dark brick buildings, most of which dated back 40 years or more, the successors and survivors of Baltimore's most traumatic event, the Great Fire of 1904. In truth, to many outsiders and some natives too, much of the city's downtown had an unimpressive, seedy look, particularly as one went south toward the Inner Harbor, then called the Basin, and Camden Station areas. The average person noticed only a few memorable landmarks — the Bromo-Seltzer Tower, the Tower building, and the dazzling Art-Deco Baltimore Trust building which is now the Maryland National Bank building. Most of the rest seemed to merge into a clutter of undistinguished low-rise commercial structures.

Or so it seemed at the time. Ironically, some are considered lost treasures now, notably the collection of nineteenth century iron-front warehouses serving the teeming wholesale produce district east of Camden Station. But then, Baltimore merely felt a bit embarrassed by the large amounts of masonry flotsam left over from its more vigorous youth.

Regardless of what downtown looked like, it was well populated. It had little competition. With no expressways, there were no suburban office parks or shopping malls. True, a few suburban shopping centers had appeared, but they were close-in, cozy

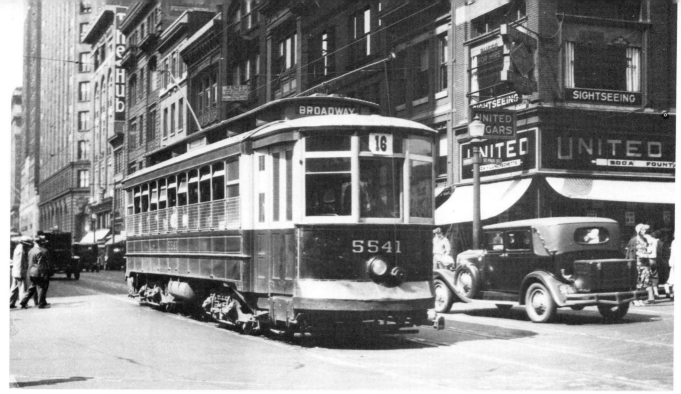

Gutted by the Great Fire of 1904, downtown Baltimore quickly rebuilt, then changed little over the next four decades. Its trolleys seemed equally ageless. This scene on Baltimore Street at the intersection of St. Paul and Light Streets dates to the mid-1930s, but it looked much the same after World War I and after World War II. One block behind No. 5541, working the #16 line to Fells Point, is the city's traditional "hub", Baltimore and Charles Streets, marked appropriately enough by The Hub department store and the Baltimore & Ohio Railroad's general office building.

and neighborly. Edmondson Village, the first "large" center, was still two years away. For any serious shopping, people came downtown to the cluster of big department stores at Howard and Lexington Streets and the specialty shops along Charles. These were not just the center of the retailing world, they *were* the world. Suburban branches were unknown and suburban competition was virtually nil.

People also usually came into town for first-run movies, and in this pre-television time they certainly saw more movies of all kinds. At least eight major theaters sat close to the Howard-Lexington hub. Grandest was the Stanley on Howard Street, followed closely by Keith's and by Loew's "twin" Century/Valencia on Lexington Street and the Hippodrome on Eutaw. Oddly, one of today's surviving movie palaces, the Town Theater on Fayette, was then doing duty as a garage. Ford's Theater on Fayette fairly well monopolized the "legitimate" theater productions. And there were neighborhood movie theaters everywhere—sometimes two or three in the same block—including such sumptuous newcomers as the Senator on York Road and the Ambassador on Liberty Heights Avenue.

Out-of-town travelers usually stayed downtown too. In 1945, the word "motel" still conjured up a picture of tacky little cabins along Route 1 to Washington or Route 40 to the northeast. Most Baltimore visitors headed for one of the four big city hotels—the Lord Baltimore which was the businessman's favorite, the Emerson, the Southern, or that durable dowager the Belvedere. The Mt. Royal, near Penn Station, also had its following although it was somewhat remote from the city's heart. The atmospheric old Rennert had been demolished four years before, but by then it had ceased to be a significant part of the commercial hotel scene.

Travelers, both natives and outsiders, had a lively and diverse transportation system to choose from. Long-distance trips usually meant the train, of course. Baltimore's two major railroads, the Baltimore & Ohio and the Pennsylvania, competed across the board with services to New York, Chicago, St. Louis, Detroit and most other eastern and midwestern points. But for Baltimoreans, B&O naturally was the preferred route unless there was some compelling reason. In going to New York, the

Pennsy's electrified "big red subway" was more frequent, faster and more convenient, yet the B&O's genteel *Royal Blue* had a regular clientele.

Depending on where they were going, train travelers used no less than six downtown terminals. Most, of course, boarded at B&O's Camden or Mt. Royal Stations, or the Pennsy's Penn Station. But patrons bound for certain local points also went to Calvert Station to catch the Pennsy's Parkton locals, Hillen Station where the Western Maryland Railway left for Glyndon, Westminster and Hagerstown, and the Maryland & Pennsylvania Railroad's anonymous little shed below the viaducts at North Avenue and Howard Street. The "Ma & Pa" always lived in a backwater of the railroad world, but did offer a scenic, leisurely ride to places like Towson, Glenarm, Bel Air, Delta and York. Few people made the trip all the way to York, though, because the Pennsy got there much faster.

The Washington, Baltimore & Annapolis high speed electric line had been gone ten years, but its big terminal at Howard and Lombard Streets still stood, complete with its platforms, tracks and a large wall sign advertising WB&A services. The WB&A's surviving segment, the Baltimore & Annapolis Railroad, continued to run its heavy, dark red electric trains from Camden Station to Bladen Street in Annapolis. B&A's big cars were beginning to show some signs of age and neglect, but they moved along fast: 55 minutes from Baltimore to Annapolis, including numerous local stops. In 1984, MTA buses needed an hour and 25 minutes for the same run.

There were some other ways of getting around too. Down at the Inner Harbor, the Old Bay Line's overnight Norfolk steamers departed from decaying but ornate piers on Light Street opposite the McCormick building. Also leaving from Light Street was the Pennsylvania Railroad's Love Point ferry, the survivor of a onetime water-rail route from Baltimore to Salisbury and Ocean City on the Eastern Shore. Ever practical, the Pennsy had recognized the inevitable and converted the ferry primarily to an auto carrier. "Smokey Joe", as the Love Point ferry was called, took a leisurely two hours and 20 minutes to cross Chesapeake Bay. If nothing else, it was relaxing. But Smokey Joe and the Sandy Point-Matapeake ferries were the only ways to "drive" to the Eastern Shore unless one went "around the Horn" through Havre de Grace and Elkton. The Bay Bridge was still in the future.

On the other side of the Baltimore harbor near Dundalk, DC-3 airliners flew from Harbor Field, the municipal airport. It is now Dundalk Marine Terminal. But airplanes were a fairly minor method of going places. Air travel was expensive and

H. H. Harwood, Jr.

Between 1935 and their demise in February of 1950, Baltimore & Annapolis Railroad interurban trains shared B&O's Camden Station which bustled with steam and diesel-hauled passenger trains for Philadelphia, New York, Washington and major points west. On this afternoon in 1947, a B&A Annapolis train and B&O Washington local leave simultaneously. The electric cars left the B&O main line near Monroe Street.

Baltimore was not a major point in the networks of the trunk airlines.

However you traveled out of town, you usually took the trolley to get to places in the city. Autos were fewer, driving more difficult, and almost everything worthwhile was on a car line anyway. There were fewer routes than today's MTA bus system, but those of 1945 carried more people and ran more often.

Indeed, streetcars seemed to be everywhere. A total of 29 separate lines still operated in 1945, including branches and shuttle services. Car tracks crisscrossed downtown in a tight thicket and reached out to such suburban spots as Ellicott City, Catonsville, Woodlawn, Cheswolde, Lake Roland, Towson, Parkville and Overlea. To the southeast and south, they ran to Sparrows Point and Fort Howard (and in the summer to Bay Shore Park), Curtis Bay, Fairfield and Westport. Once the cars had roamed even farther: to Reisterstown and Glyndon, Pikesville, Halethorpe, Carney and Middle River. But during the Depression years, these light-traffic rural routes had been switched to feeder buses.

The fare, incidentally, was ten cents—exact change not required. Cheap, you may think, but at that time a clerk in the B&O's general offices earned about $8 a day and the "$10,000-a-year-man" was the symbol of salaried success.

The streetcar system not only was big and busy, but had almost every sort of scenery, construction type and operational method. Once outside the city center, many routes ran over private open track, which was both traffic-free and pretty. Sometimes this was laid in grassy boulevard median strips, sometimes it followed the side of the road, and sometimes it struck out through woods and fields on its own. Examples were almost too numerous to catalog: Outer Edmondson Avenue, Gwynn Oak Avenue and Harford Road by Clifton Park all had long stretches of roadside right-of-way. Roland Avenue, Liberty Heights Avenue and Dundalk Avenue had varying types of center-boulevard track. The Mt. Washington-Pimlico and Windsor Hills-Dickeyville areas had a little bit of everything. Upper St. Paul Street in Guilford had a trolley layout almost unique in the country, carefully designed to fit the aesthetics of this rarified community. The two tracks of the #11 line to Bedford Square were split, with a separate track on each side of the roadway set in a private reservation and bordered by a well-trimmed hedge.

In fact, many lines were worth riding strictly to savor their scenery or operating peculiarities. The high speed, high capacity Dundalk-Sparrows Point route looked much like a mainline railroad with its straight open track, block signals, train operation, its long Bear Creek trestle and industrial surroundings. In a somewhat similar environment, Point Breeze cars picked their way through a puzzle of railroad tracks and manufacturing plants in the Canton area. At the other extreme was the bucolic Dickeyville-Lorraine line, whose single track meandered through woods, along roadsides and streams, and through the center of a tiny early nineteenth century mill village. All of that, incidentally, was inside the Baltimore city limits. Ellicott City trolleys ran cross-country west of Rolling Road, cutting through a high hill and rumbling over the Patapsco River on a long steel truss bridge. And at the north end of the city, streetcar riders also could commune with unspoiled woods, streams and ponds on their way to Lakeside loop near Lake Roland. In yet another kind of world was the lone shuttle car plodding over four blocks of Union Avenue in Woodberry, carrying workers from Hampden and the Falls Road car line down the steep hill to the old mills in the Jones Falls valley.

Then there were several spectacular bridges and viaducts. Most memorable was the Guilford Avenue "elevated", running for over three-quarters of a mile above Guilford between Lexington and Chase Streets. Almost as awesome was the Huntington Avenue trestle, which hurdled the Stony Run valley between the north end of Huntington Avenue and 33rd and Keswick in Hampden. And at the southeastern corner of the system, Sparrows Point cars crossed the wide expanse of Bear Creek estuary on a long low timber trestle punctuated by a steel swing bridge at its center. East of Sparrows Point, other wood trestles carried an extension of the line over inlets on its way to Fort Howard and Bay Shore.

Populating this streetcar Garden of Eden was a fleet of 1,040 operating trolleys, most of which were as atmospheric as the lines on which they ran. They were a mishmash of ages, designs and color schemes, with almost a 40-year spread between the newest and oldest cars. Most were old.

Newest in the fleet were 275 sleek PCC streamliners dating from the 1936 to 1944 period. Unquestionably the finest in trolley technology, these were the product of a joint street railway industry group called the Electric Railway President's Conference Committee. Named for this committee, the PCC cars were smooth, fast and quiet, at least by streetcar standards. All were painted in an attractive deep blue-green and cream combination with orange trim.

Almost as young in years, having been built in 1930, but less advanced or as esthetic as the PCC's, were 150 steel cars known in the trade as Peter

Witts. The odd name honored a Cleveland public official who had designed their floor layout and original fare collection system. Their bright yellow and cream paint, set off with a red band, helped relieve their rather severe squared-off looks.

But the dominant Baltimore streetcar was a wood-bodied ancient-appearing ark called the Brill semi-convertible. Its classic turn-of-the-century design dated to 1905, although some were as new as 1919. By 1945, they were mechanically and visually obsolete, but also charming provided you didn't have to ride them regularly. Indeed, to some outsiders they helped reinforce Baltimore's image of decaying gentility. The old Brills came in two color schemes: red and cream for two-man cars which passengers entered at the rear, and a pleasant yellow and cream with thin red striping for one-man cars. Some of the two-man cars were fitted for train operation and often ran in two- and three-car sets on the heavy Sparrows Point line where they were affectionately known as the "red rockets". The Brill semi-convertibles may have been old, but they were hardy and numerous. Over 570 of them still whined and clattered over the streets in 1945, and you were likely to see them on almost every line at one time or another.

Rounding out the roster were 43 odd two-unit articulated cars, one of the very few fleets of articulateds ever regularly used on American street railways. At first glance, these looked much like the Brill semi-convertibles and were painted in the same yellow and cream colors, but they were unmistakably their own breed. Looking like a two-car train which wasn't fully hatched, they were impressive and fascinating to watch as they swallowed up crowds or negotiated curves. The articulateds had been home-built from old semi-convertibles and obsolete open car bodies, an inventive way of getting extra rush hour capacity cheap. But by 1945, their ranks were thinning and the operable survivors were confined to only four or five lines at various peak hours.

Motor buses were strongly in evidence, of course, but you saw surprisingly few of them in the downtown area. There were only three trunk bus routes in 1945. Most of the remaining lines radiated from trolley terminals to reach newly-developed or lightly-populated outlying areas. These feeder buses served such spots as Pikesville, Reisterstown-Glyndon, Randallstown, Homeland, Northwood, Carney, and the war-created housing developments at Middle River and Armistead Gardens. Riding them usually was a bit of a nuisance, since you generally had to transfer to a streetcar to get anywhere. For example, anyone going downtown from Homeland rode a Route "O" bus to Bedford Square and changed to the #11 trolley. Northwood residents took the "T" bus to 33rd and Greenmount where they waited for a #8 car, which they hoped was not too crowded. Several independent bus companies also operated to various suburban points from downtown or from the ends of car lines.

There also was a third variety of transit vehicle in Baltimore, the trackless trolley. These bus-trolley hybrids were very smooth, quiet, and all things considered, probably the most pleasant to ride of anything in Baltimore, past or present—at least on smooth pavement. There were three trackless trolley routes in 1945, all of them onetime streetcar lines. More would come soon to replace other car lines, but sadly, all would be gone before the last streetcar ran.

The events leading up to that last streetcar started in 1945 and moved quickly afterwards. Although Baltimore's transit scene in 1945 was active and atmospheric, there were many problems below the surface. The worst was money. For although Baltimore had been a premier streetcar city, it was never very profitable for the streetcar operators. The system was then operated by the Baltimore Transit Company, a private concern which in 1945 was only ten years old. BTC was the Depression-born reincarnation of the bankrupt United Railways & Electric Company, originally formed in 1899 to consolidate and modernize Baltimore's diverse independent streetcar companies. Prosperity always had eluded the "United" and so far BTC had been no luckier. It was now struggling with an aging streetcar fleet and obsolete track layout, both of which had been badly battered by the wartime crush.

At the same time, the transit company faced the need to serve the growing areas beyond and between the car lines, and to generally adapt its route system to a changing city. And with the war's end, patronage quickly resumed the long downward slide which had started 20 years before. The drastic drop created a cash flow crisis just as this modernization was most demanded. By then, it also seemed clear that the economics of streetcar operation were questionable, even if the capital could be found to rebuild the lines and replace the cars.

Two events speeded the end of the streetcars. First, in 1945, working control of Baltimore Transit was taken over by Chicago-based National City Lines, a bus-minded holding company which specialized in modernizing ailing trolley operations. Second was the arrival of Henry Barnes, the creative, aggressive and controversial traffic commissioner hired to unclog the city's snarled streets. Barnes's one-way street systems, expanded traffic

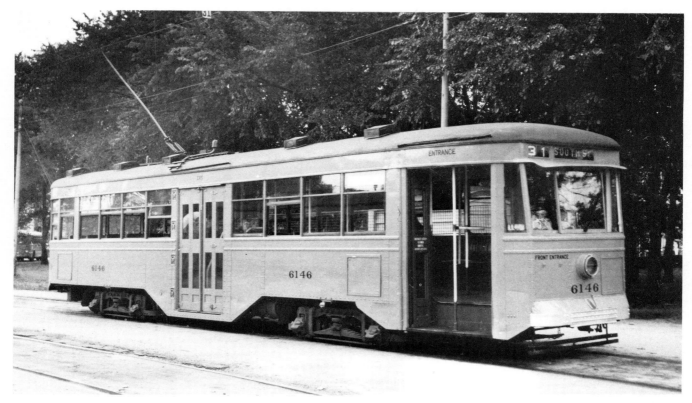

M. E. Borgnis

Contemporaneous with the Model A Ford, Baltimore's Peter Witt cars shared the same no-frills design philosophy. The unadorned, bland orange-yellow color scheme used after 1949 gave them an even more utilitarian look. But by 1930 standards they were fast and comfortable—and certainly an exhilarating change from the omnipresent, archaic semi-convertibles. Peter Witt was a famous Cleveland politician and onetime traction commissioner who had patented a fast-loading fare collection system and car floor plan. Passengers entered at the front, left by the center door, and paid when they passed a conductor stationed by the center door. Because of labor costs, the UR&E quickly abandoned the Witt system and converted the cars to one-man operation, but the name stuck. No. 6146, a 1930 Brill product, rests at Belvedere loop in 1950.

lanes and free-flow concepts simply were incompatible with tracks and trolleys.

Buses seemed the solution to everyone's problems. Clearly they were more flexible, considerably cheaper to buy and run, and required no commitments to right-of-way maintenance or paving. Equally important, they offered an excellent hedge against the uncertainties of declining business and shifting riding patterns. It was, after all, a generation before OPEC or air pollution concerns.

And so on June 22, 1947, the first wave of bus substitutions began. On that date four north Baltimore lines ended, victims of the conversion of St. Paul, Charles and Calvert Streets to one-way traffic. More changeovers came quickly. Eleven years later only two trolley routes remained: the heavily-used #8 Towson-Catonsville and #15 Overlea-Walbrook Junction lines. Their passenger volume and the lack of money for enough bus replacements brought a brief reprieve, but the inevitable finally came in the bleak pre-dawn hours of Sunday, November 3, 1963. In the meantime, all those expressways, malls, office parks and urban redevelopments were under way or already completed.

Baltimore not only was no longer a streetcar city, but never could be again.

DOWNTOWN

Downtown Baltimore was a confusing and noisy mishmash of rails, crossings and switches. Virtually every street carried car tracks and a wide variety of routings and loops was possible. Each line seemed to follow a different path through the area, with some looping downtown, others terminating on the outer fringes, and still others running through.

Both, E. S. Miller

[ABOVE:] **The #18 Canton-Pennsylvania Avenue line was one which ran through, using Lombard and Saratoga Streets. Here semi-convertible No. 5742 swings onto Saratoga Street from Eutaw in June 1951 on its way to Pennsylvania and North Avenues. A line maintenance crew rests at the curbside waiting for a lull in the streetcar traffic. [LEFT:] Four blocks east on Saratoga, PCC No. 7084 handles a #14 Edmondson Avenue run. It waits to turn south on Charles to complete a terminal loop which will take it back west on Lexington. The classic 1908 Metropolitan Savings Bank building on the left was sacrificed to the Charles Center redevelopment in 1963, but happily the other buildings in this 1949 scene have been preserved and restored.**

E. S. Miller

[ABOVE:] **Part of the same loop as used by the Edmondson Avenue cars was this switch at Lexington Street and Park Avenue. A #4 line car, No. 5806, prepares to turn north on Park in November 1949. Since then, Keith's Theater has been razed for a parking garage, and the entranceway remodeled into a store. The nondescript buildings behind the streetcar on Liberty have disappeared for Charles Center. Lexington Street itself is now a pedestrian mall.** [BELOW:] **To the south, a car on line #33 from West Arlington makes its terminal loop in front of the B&O's grimy Camden Station in 1946 just as a trackless trolley from Morrell Park bounces by on the stone paving. Although the hotel and other buildings on the left are gone, Camden Station was cleaned up in 1951 and still looks considerably improved.**

G. J. Voith

Typical of vanished downtown Baltimore are the scenes on these two pages. [ABOVE:] The First National Bank building standing tall in the rear is the only present day landmark to place this 1950 scene of an outbound Garrison Boulevard PCC running west on Redwood Street at Hopkins Place. All the immediate surroundings have been removed and replaced with the Hopkins Plaza complex, while the photo itself is taken from the site of the Civic Center. [BELOW:] Three blocks south on Hopkins Place where it becomes Sharp Street, the 1950 scene looked like this as Peter Witt No. 6125 prepared to turn west onto Camden Street. The Convention Center is now to the far right.

Both, E. S. Miller

E. S. Miller

[ABOVE:] **Two blocks further south, PCC No. 7065 makes its way south on Sharp Street at Conway heading for a loop at Light and Lee Streets. To the left in this 1950 view are the B&O's public freight delivery tracks, now a parking lot. The buildings to the right have been cleared for Convention Center area redevelopment. Still punctuating the Baltimore skyline is the perennial Bromo-Seltzer Tower.** [BELOW:] **Curtis Bay-bound Peter Witt No. 6047 is briefly stymied at Baltimore and Light Streets by someone's bright new 1947 Nash which, apparently, can't retreat. The car line was in its last year, to be replaced the following March by yellow-green-and-light gray GM buses like the interloper on the right. Thirty-five years later rails returned to this spot, but underground. It is now the site of MTA Metro's Charles Center terminal. All the buildings behind the car are now gone; the last, the stolid 1930 Union Trust Company came down in late 1983.**

G. J. Voith

[LEFT:] **During the late 1940s, #26 Sparrows Point cars came into downtown on Lombard Street and looped at Pearl, west of the city's center. Heading east on Lombard, a pair of Sparrows Point "red rockets" clatters over the five-point intersection with Howard and Liberty Streets in May of 1948. To the left was the WB&A's Baltimore terminal. Although the last WB&A interurban ran 13 years before, the name was kept alive by a restaurant in the building.** [BELOW:] **Inbound semi-convertible No. 5853 rolls past a portable traffic control booth on Lombard at South Street in September 1949. At the time, several major downtown intersections were still manually controlled. This one rated only part-time police coverage, and the booth was rolled away in light periods.**

R. W. Janssen

E. S. Miller

A two-car Sparrows Point train taxes the trusses of the 1877 Lombard Street bridge over Jones Falls in 1950. The bridge long outlasted the cars, finally being replaced about 1973 but its members have been preserved for eventual re-erection. In addition to vehicles, the unique bridge also carried a water main, visible behind the rear car to the left. Baltimore's most famous industrial relic, the 1828 Phoenix Shot Tower, pokes up in the rear, three blocks north. Molten lead was prepared at the top of the tower and dropped into water-filled receivers at the bottom to form perfect spheres for shot.

E. S. Miller

Streetcars were nearing the end in this October 1963 view, but the durable Shot Tower still dominates the downtown scene. PCC's running on lines #8 (near) and #15 (distant) simultaneously swing onto Fayette Street in the City Hall area. By then the complex trackwork at Holliday Street in the foreground was only partly used to turn back certain #8 cars. The old central police headquarters in the rear was demolished in 1984, but the stolid Mussolini-style War Memorial building apparently will stand forever.

F. W. Schneider, III

An inbound #8 line PCC rolls down Hillen Street past the Western Maryland Railway's 1875 Hillen Station complex. When this 1950 photo was taken, the WM still ran two cleanly maintained Hagerstown locals and a commuter run to Union Bridge. Most passengers, however, boarded them at better-located Penn Station. The Victorian terminal complex came down in 1954, replaced by a mundane warehouse, and the WM ran its last Baltimore passenger train in 1957.

E. S. Miller

G. J. Voith

Watched over by an ornate "bishop's crook" street lamp, outbound articulated No. 8124 negotiates the switch at Hillen and Forrest Streets carrying an afternoon rush hour crowd on the heavy Greenmount Avenue-York Road route. Seen here about 1945, these unique arks would be gone within three years.

E. S. Miller

Inbound on Gay Street, a dark green PCC on the #15 Belair Road line nears Lexington. Most buildings in this May 1950 scene have been leveled for the Jones Falls Expressway extension which now bridges Gay Street a block behind the car. One of the buildings on the left, however, still survives as a Baltimore railfan haven—the M. B. Klein hobby store.

Baltimore Transit acquired a new, albeit short piece of private right-of-way in 1941 when the Latrobe Homes urban renewal project swallowed up a block of Ashland Avenue between Aisquith and Ensor Streets. The street was closed, but the car line was continued on the old alignment within the new housing development. PCC No. 7355 heads into town at Ensor Street.

E. S. Miller

GUILFORD AVENUE ELEVATED

The famous Guilford Avenue "elevated" was the fastest, most direct but least utilized of the major downtown routes. Sometimes called the "viadock" in Baltimorese, it was originally built in 1892 to 1893 by the Lake Roland Elevated Railway, the transit adjunct of the Roland Park residential development. As a latecomer to Baltimore's transit scene, the Lake Roland line was forced to use Guilford Avenue which already was occupied by the Northern Central Railway (later the Pennsylvania Railroad) tracks reaching Calvert Station and various warehouses. Thus the viaduct was necessary to hurdle the railroad activity. However, the route lay on the fringes of the commercial and residential areas, and for most of its life it carried lighter density car lines. In June of 1947, the heavy #8 Towson-Catonsville line was rerouted onto the "el", but in January 1950 service reverted to Greenmount Avenue and the structure was closed and dismantled.

[LEFT:] The south end of the "el" came to earth in the block between Saratoga and Lexington Streets. Green PCC No. 7026 descends the ramp on its long trip from Towson to Catonsville in June 1948.

G. J. Voith

17

Both, E. S. Miller

The Guilford Avenue elevated's 4,000 foot length is evident in the two views on the opposite page, both taken from the Orleans Street viaduct in September 1949. [OPPOSITE TOP:] Looking south, a Towson-bound PCC pulls away from the Pleasant Street station. Railroad sidings served many of the now-removed commercial buildings alongside. [OPPOSITE BOTTOM:] Looking north, an inbound #8 line car passes steelwork for the new Sunpapers building. A year before, the site had been occupied by the Northern Central Railway's 1850 Calvert Station, that railroad's onetime Baltimore terminal. But in 1949, Parkton locals on the Northern Central route ran from the line's 1865 freight house, seen a block behind the PCC car.

"El" stations were spartan affairs. Madison Street was typical. [THIS PAGE TOP:] It's shown here topside as a southbound Irvington car glides into the station. The fan-shaped iron barrier in the foreground was meant to discourage anyone from short-cutting over the girders. It was tried at least once, with a fatal result. [THIS PAGE MIDDLE:] From below it is clear why Guilford Avenue was hard to navigate on the surface. [THIS PAGE BOTTOM:] The less recorded north end was at Chase Street, seen in 1949 as PCC No. 7033 came cautiously down. On its way to Towson, it will use Guilford as far as North Avenue, then turn east to Greenmount.

E. S. Miller

G. J. Voith

E. S. Miller

Both, E. S. Miller

A few lines skirted the downtown area but did not enter. Heaviest was the #13 North Avenue crosstown line running from Walbrook to Gay Street and crossing a multitude of radial routes in the process. Several other car lines used sections of North Avenue on their way in and out of downtown. [ABOVE:] Typical of North Avenue transfer points was Linden Avenue. The camera looks west in September 1949 as an inbound PCC from Garrison Boulevard loads. Urban renewal now has left this area mostly barren, although the one-story block on the right remains. The Linden Theater, however, closed and was converted to other uses. [BELOW:] Eastbound #13 line PCC No. 7414 comes off the North Avenue bridge at Howard Street. The stairway behind the 1947 Packard on the left led down to the "Ma & Pa" railroad terminal, a spartan little shed which had sufficed since the railroad's attractive stone street-level station was demolished in 1937 to make way for the Howard Street viaduct. In the haze behind the auto is the also-departed Mt. Royal water pumping station, sacrificed for the Jones Falls Expressway.

The North Avenue Market was built in 1928 for the uptown trade. No. 5682 working eastbound on the #13 line pauses near this active community center at Maryland Avenue.

Another "fringe" route was the #30 Fremont Avenue line, circling the west side of the city from North Avenue and Charles to south Baltimore. In this November 1949 view, PCC No. 7135 pauses at Fremont and Edmondson Avenues on its roundabout way to South Charles and Barney Streets. Painted on the street is a warning to motorists that the streetcars overhang when turning.

F. W. Schneider, III

Row houses, trees and trolleys—these were Baltimore in the first half of the twentieth century. It was October 1963 and the trolleys were in their last month as battered PCC No. 7418 makes its way east on Edmondson Avenue at Schroeder Street. The car is running on a gerrymandered #15 Overlea-Belair Road-Walbrook Junction line, patched together in 1954 from parts of the onetime #4 Edmondson Avenue-Walbrook Junction and #15 Belair Road-West Baltimore Street lines.

WESTERN SUBURBAN LINES

● **Irvington** ● **Edmondson Village** ● **Catonsville** ● **Ellicott City** ●

Two lines reached west to Catonsville—the west end of the famous #8 Towson-Catonsville line, running via Frederick Road, and the #9-14 line along Edmondson Avenue which went on to Ellicott City. Frederick Road was the busier, passing through Irvington and Catonsville's commercial center, but Edmondson Avenue was the prettier with its tree-bordered private track serving well-tended residential areas. The Ellicott City extension (the #9 section of the #9-14 hybrid) was downright backwoods west of Rolling Road where the #14 cars looped. It was almost totally away from civilization until it came out into the Patapsco River valley.

H. H. Harwood, Jr.

A major operating center for the Frederick Road line was this 1898 carhouse at Collins Avenue in Irvington, shown at the end of its life in November 1963. The relic outlived many more modern carhouses on the Baltimore system and was one of the last two in service when the last streetcar ran. Unfortunately it was subsequently demolished.

Both, E. S. Miller

[TOP LEFT:] **On its way to Catonsville amid typical Frederick Road surroundings, No. 7380 passes Shady Nook Avenue, just east of the present Beltway interchange. The date was May 1951.** [TOP RIGHT:] **West of the center of Catonsville, the original #8 line alignment followed the north side of Frederick Road on a private right-of-way. As part of a 1951 street widening project, the tracks were relocated to the center in what was to be one of the last major streetcar line reconstruction projects. In this scene taken at Stanley Drive in May of that year, the job was half done. An eastbound #8 PCC rolls over the new line while the old westbound track is barely visible on its alignment at the far right.** [LEFT:] **For its finale, the #8 line swung north from Frederick Road near Montrose Avenue and plunged into the woods for a brief run to its terminal at Edmondson Avenue. Towson-bound No. 7364 is nearing Frederick Road in August 1963.**

H. H. Harwood, Jr.

Both, E. S. Miller

[ABOVE:] **The Edmondson Avenue route generally passed through more newly-built areas, and in the late 1940s Baltimore's newest and most exciting development was the "big" Edmondson Village shopping center seen here in January 1951. Eastbound No. 7081 pauses opposite the center's Georgian Revival-style theater. The line along this section of Edmondson Avenue was set in a private center reservation. [RIGHT:] Farther west, Edmondson Avenue was purely residential, with the car line following the south side of a pleasant two-lane roadway. Semi-convertible No. 5680 is heading for Ellicott City near Laurel Hill Lane in the North Bend area early in 1951.**

[ABOVE:] **It's early in April 1951, and greenery is sprouting along with the Academy Heights development. Heights home buyers could catch the #14 trolley for town, such as PCC No. 7377 swinging around the bend of Edmondson Avenue at Nunnery Lane.** [RIGHT:] **A short distance to the west, the countryside was almost unspoiled. On the same spring day, a semi-convertible bound for Ellicott City passes Harlem Lane. The area directly ahead of the car is now the interchange with the Beltway.**

26

[ABOVE:] **Edmondson Avenue and Ingleside, on the outskirts of Catonsville, looked like a country crossroads in 1951. Car No. 7378 is outbound for the Rolling Road loop. Just around the curve to its rear is the present day Beltway interchange.** [RIGHT:] **Edmondson Avenue skirts the north side of "old" Catonsville, then as now an area of large homes and lots of trees. In this view near Glenmore Avenue, PCC No. 7377 is returning from Rolling Road to its downtown terminal at Charles and Lexington Streets. In the far distance, an Ellicott City car follows it into town.**

Both, E. S. Miller

[ABOVE:] **Edmondson and Dutton Avenues, locally called Catonsville Junction, was a small commercial center serving northwest Catonsville and a key trolley transfer point. Out of the picture on the left was the end of the #8 Towson-Catonsville line. Passengers between Frederick Road points and Rolling Road, Oella and Ellicott City changed cars here. Some Ellicott City runs also switched back here; downtown riders took either #8 or #14 cars. The bucktoothed 1950 Buick by the Caton Tavern was one year old as a Rolling Road PCC followed an ancient Ellicott City semi-convertible west. After the demise of the Edmondson Avenue line in September of 1954, isolated Ellicott City shuttle cars continued running from this point for another ten months before they too died.** [BELOW:] **Between Catonsville Junction and Rolling Road, the car tracks occupied the center of Edmondson Avenue, such as here at Oakdale Avenue. Just ahead of the westbound Ellicott City car is Rolling Road loop, the turnback point for the #14 line cars.**

Both, E. S. Miller

[ABOVE:] **The same Ellicott City-bound car, No. 5772, pauses briefly at Rolling Road loop waiting station before plunging ahead into the woods. The terminal was located just west of the Edmondson Avenue and Rolling Road intersection. This section of the old trolley right-of-way has since been paved over as an extension of Edmondson Avenue.** [BELOW:] **The farther west the Ellicott City car went, the deeper the woods got—or so it seemed. This was typical of the scenery as the line dropped into the Patapsco River valley. The car is westbound in April 1951.**

Both, E. S. Miller

29

Both, E. S. Miller

30

Ellicott City, a late eighteenth century flour milling town, was nestled in a gorge of the Patapsco River 14 rail miles west of Baltimore—but it really existed in another world. The B&O's pioneering strap rails reached the town in 1831 by following the river valley. The cross-country trolley line arrived in 1899. [OPPOSITE PAGE, TOP:] **Cars crossed the Patapsco on this long truss bridge, which actually carried a gauntleted double track. The Frederick turnpike crossed immediately out of the picture on the right. On the far river bank are ancient mill-workers' houses and the wilderness right-of-way uphill to Catonsville. Ellicott City's Main Street lies ahead of semi-convertible No. 5767 as it rolls off the trestle into town in April 1951.** [OPPOSITE PAGE, BOTTOM:] **Main Street, a part of the old Frederick turnpike, passed under the B&O's line just west of the river bridges. The steel railroad girder bridge framing cars No. 5727 and No. 5745 is a second-generation replacement for the original triple-arch stone Oliver viaduct. Built in 1831, the viaduct was partially removed in 1868, but the stone center pier was left in place until the 1930s. The wide swing of the eastbound car track at the left was needed to clear the pier, an alignment that was never adjusted.**

[RIGHT:] **Crammed into a narrow tributary valley at a right angle to the Patapsco River, Ellicott City always had a peculiarly European look with its steep hillsides and closely-packed stone buildings. In a 1947 view west from the B&O bridge, red and cream No. 5292 grinds up Main Street to its Fells Lane terminal, pursued by a rumbleseated roadster.**

R. M. Vogel

31

NORTHWEST SUBURBAN LINES

- Walbrook • Windsor Hills • Dickeyville •
- Lorraine Cemetery • Ashburton • Gwynn Oak Park •
- Woodlawn • West Arlington • Belvedere • Park Heights •

Walbrook, at the west end of North Avenue, started as a late nineteenth century suburban development but quickly grew after it became a hub for several trolley lines reaching out of the city to northwestern points. [ABOVE:] It's a quiet Sunday noon in the center of Walbrook as No. 7409 heads east on North Avenue in January 1951. At this time three neighborhood theaters populated this block: the Walbrook on the right and the Windsor and the Hilton on the left. The Windsor and Hilton closed in the 1950s, while the grandiose Walbrook built in 1916 lasted until 1964. All three still stand, converted to other uses, the Walbrook as a church.

[BOTTOM:] **Walbrook Junction, four blocks northwest at Clifton Avenue and Garrison Boulevard was an active terminal and transfer point. In the late 1940s, four lines came together here: #4 Edmondson Avenue (which continued to Windsor Hills), #13 North Avenue, #31 Garrison Boulevard and the picturesque #35 line to Lorraine Cemetery via Dickeyville. This view looks northwest at the Clifton and Garrison intersection in mid-1950. To the right, green No. 7001, Baltimore's first PCC, is inbound from Garrison Boulevard while No. 7419 wearing a National City Lines "fruit salad" yellow-green-and-light gray paint scheme has made its loop at the junction terminal and prepares to start east on a North Avenue run. [BELOW:] Walbrook Junction loop itself lay in the triangle bounded by Clifton Avenue and Windsor Mill Road. The camera looks along Windsor Mill as another North Avenue car makes ready to leave.**

All, E. S. Miller

E. S. Miller

West of Walbrook Junction, the #35 Lorraine line shared track with the #4 line as far as Windsor Hills, following Clifton Avenue through tree-shaded residential areas. In a prototypical streetcar scene, semi-convertible No. 5680 is outbound on Clifton Avenue at Allendale Road in July 1950.

[ABOVE:] **No. 5622 is inbound for Walbrook Junction on Clifton at Mt. Holly.** [BELOW:] **Windsor Hills was a turn-of-the-century "garden suburb", laid out with winding streets, large houses, and lots of woods. The trolley fitted right in. No. 5622 is westbound for Lorraine at Clifton and Queen Anne Road in July 1950. The line itself was opened in 1904, contemporaneous with the development.**

Both, E. S. Miller

Both, *E. S. Miller*

R. W. Janssen

Beyond Windsor Hills, the Lorraine line got progressively more rural—and went farther backwards in time. These views, all taken between 1948 and 1950, trace the route between Windsor Hills and Dickeyville. [TOP:] Inbound No. 5622 approaches Oakdale Top station near Clifton and Queen Anne Road. [MIDDLE:] Double track ended at Clifton and Prospect Circle. Outbound No. 5680 begins the descent into the Gwynns Falls valley. [BOTTOM:] Near Fairfax Road, deep woods surrounded the cars. A light snowfall dampens the clatter of No. 5395 as it returns from Gwynns Falls and Dickeyville.

[TOP:] **Double track resumed briefly at the little truss bridge over Gwynns Falls, the stream which once provided power for mills which first appeared in this area in 1762. This view looks west toward Wetheredsville Road (Dickeyville's earlier name) as eastbound No. 5680 waits for its meet with a westbound car.** [MIDDLE:] **West of the bridge, the trolley tracks played tag with Wetheredsville Road, swinging from south side to center to north side as they approached Dickeyville. No. 5622 is on its way to Walbrook Junction in July 1950.** [BOTTOM:] **Trolley riders literally were taken back over 100 years as the cars entered Dickeyville, a tiny mill town which grew up in the late 1700s and early 1800s, then froze in time. It still remains an isolated gem, superbly restored, inside Baltimore's city limits. In this atmospheric scene, which could be New England circa 1905, eastbound No. 5727 follows Wetheredsville Road as a mill worker returns home in mid-afternoon.**

Both, E. S. Miller

J. W. Vigrass

"Downtown" Dickeyville in July 1950 as Lorraine-bound No. 5680 again crosses Wetheredsville Road. Out of the photo to the left was a stub end siding and waiting shelter. In earlier years, through cars from downtown terminated here and a "jerkwater" shuttle ran to Lorraine Cemetery.

Both, E. S. Miller

Beyond Dickeyville, the Lorraine route described a series of broad "S" curves as it worked its way alongside Forest Park Avenue, Windsor Mill Road, Kernan Drive and Dogwood Road to reach the cemetery. Here inbound No. 5622 swings into the curve connecting Windsor Mill and Forest Park, passing the gates of Kernan Hospital, a famous children's orthopedic and rehabilitation center.

[ABOVE:] **Baltimore's last major streetcar trunk line extension was the route out Liberty Heights Avenue from Reisterstown Road to Gwynn Oak Avenue, opened in 1917. For most of its life it carried #32 Woodlawn cars, although after June of 1948, the West Arlington line also was routed into town over Liberty Heights. On the last day of service, September 3, 1955, PCC No. 7343 rolls downgrade at Wabash Avenue. Lake Ashburton is to the left.** [BELOW:] **Locally known as Gwynn Oak Junction, the intersection of Liberty Heights and Gwynn Oak Avenues was the dividing point for branches to Woodlawn (right) and West Arlington-Belvedere (left). Bracketed by the 1933 Gwynn Theater and Moderne 1935 Ambassador Theater, outbound Peter Witt No. 6120 takes the switch for Woodlawn. The two theaters are long since closed, the Gwynn having done so shortly after this April 1951 photo was taken. Both remain in other uses. Another view of this junction appears on page 41.**

G. J. Voith

[THIS PAGE, TOP] **The outstanding landmark on the Woodlawn line—and a major Baltimore tradition for over 70 years—was Gwynn Oak Park. Set in a sylvan spot along Gwynns Falls, the park began in the 1890s and was owned by the trolley company for much of its life. In the Woodlawn line's last summer, yellow-orange Peter Witt No. 6119 passes the park's roller coaster in August 1955. Gwynn Oak Park finally closed in 1974 and burned the following year, yet No. 6119 still survives at the Baltimore Streetcar Museum.**

[THIS PAGE, BOTTOM:] **The park and the broad Gwynns Falls valley can be seen to the left of Woodlawn-bound PCC No. 7067 running alongside Gwynn Oak Avenue near Poplar Drive in April 1951. From here to Woodlawn the line originally was single track.**

[OPPOSITE PAGE, TOP:] **Returning to Gwynn Oak Junction, we now look along the West Arlington branch. Originally designated #5-33, this line came out of town on Park Heights Avenue and terminated here at Liberty Heights and Gwynn Oak. In June 1948, the Park Heights line died and West Arlington cars were routed down Liberty Heights. The junction was extra busy in April 1947 as fan excursion car No. 5566 shared tracks with two other semi-convertibles at the terminal switchback.** [OPPOSITE PAGE, BOTTOM:] **West Arlington was another turn-of-the-century residential development, mostly single homes, hedges and trees. This view is at Gwynn Oak Avenue at Post Road in April 1951. The PCC will go downtown via Liberty Heights Avenue.**

E. S. Miller

L. W. Rice

E. S. Miller

G. J. Voith

E. S. Miller

[OPPOSITE PAGE, TOP:] **On the West Arlington line, No. 5763 skims through the snow along Gwynn Oak Avenue in 1946.** [OPPOSITE PAGE, BOTTOM:] **A few blocks to the southeast in the Forest Park area, an inbound Garrison Boulevard PCC has just crossed Liberty Heights Avenue and is approaching the Berwyn Avenue intersection in May 1950. Before the inner section of the Liberty Heights trackage was opened in 1917, Woodlawn cars came out Garrison Boulevard to this point and continued on Berwyn (seen to the left) to Liberty Heights.**

G. J. Voith

Between Reisterstown Road and present Wabash Avenue, West Arlington and Garrison Boulevard cars crossed the Western Maryland Railway main line on a short private right-of-way following the line of Belvedere Avenue. In this 1947 scene, No. 5757 has received a green signal at the interlocking and is about to crash over the crossing on its way to West Arlington. Directly behind the camera is the site of today's MTA-Metro subway viaduct.

Belvedere carhouse, on Belvedere Avenue east of Reisterstown Road, was a thriving hub for northwest Baltimore car and bus lines. As late as 1948, three streetcar routes and two feeder bus lines terminated here. Across the street once was long-defunct Electric Park, later a housing development. [ABOVE:] The area looked like this in May 1950 as a PCC started west on a Garrison Boulevard run while Peter Witt No. 6021, assigned to the Mt. Washington-Pimlico line, relaxes by the ornate 1907 carhouse. [BELOW:] Just east of the carhouse was Belvedere terminal loop, substation and storage yard. Peter Witt No. 6022 is arriving from Mt. Washington while a trio of tiny Ford feeder buses sit idle by the substation.

Both, E. S. Miller

Both, G. J. Voith

[ABOVE:] **Park Heights Avenue was yet another busy northwest area trunk line carrying #5 cars to Pimlico and the #33 West Arlington route. Before 1932, #5 ran all the way to Reisterstown and Emory Grove via Park Heights, Slade Avenue and Reisterstown Road. It was then cut back in stages to a final terminal at Park Heights and Manhattan Avenue, just beyond present day Northern Parkway. Park Circle in 1947 had two landmarks—Carlin's Park (out of the photo to the left) and the highly visible Gunther's Beer sign. Gunther's, like Brill semi-convertible No. 5219 inbound at the circle, was a long-time Baltimore tradition. It lived only slightly longer than the streetcar; the Highlandtown brewery was bought by Hamm's in 1960. Baltimoreans didn't like the new taste or name, and it too disappeared. [BELOW:] At Park Heights and Belvedere, No. 5747 from West Arlington picks through the pedestrians as it heads downtown via Park Heights. The Mt. Washington-Falls Road Peter Witt behind will go straight across the intersection past Pimlico racetrack.**

FALLS ROAD - MT. WASHINGTON LINE

● Hampden ● Woodberry ● Mt. Washington ● Pimlico ● Cheswolde ●

R. W. Janssen

Easily Baltimore's most varied line was the #25 Falls Road-Mt. Washington-Pimlico. It included some Pittsburgh-style topography and a range of neighborhoods from nineteenth century millworkers' communities to Victorian suburbs to the famous Pimlico racetrack. It also had history because pieces of the route were part of Leo Daft's pioneering 1885 electric line.

[ABOVE:] **Stony Run valley is a woodsy, scenic barrier separating Hampden from downtown Baltimore. In the mid-1890s, the one-time City & Suburban Railway spanned it with this spectacular structure reaching from the end of Huntington Avenue to 33rd and Keswick in Hampden. Below was the Ma & Pa railroad's single track. The trestle is in its last month of service in April 1949 as it supports an inbound #25 line Peter Witt.** [LEFT:] **A picturesque appendage of the Falls Road line was the Union Avenue "jerkwater", a short shuttle between 36th and Roland Avenue in Hampden and the cluster of late nineteenth century textile mills and foundries in the Jones Falls valley at Woodberry. Semi-convertible No. 5765 drops down the steep Union Avenue hill into the valley, passing ancient stone mill workers' houses. This anachronism lasted until April 1949, the date of this photo.**

G. J. Voith

Gateway to Mt. Washington was the 1927 Kelly Avenue viaduct spanning Jones Falls and the Pennsylvania Railroad. Outbound PCC No. 7018 crosses in April 1949. The concrete viaduct replaced a spindly 1897 steel streetcar trestle and a grade level street crossing.

G. J. Voith

PCC No. 7001 has just crossed the Kelly Avenue viaduct and is swinging around the back side of Mt. Washington's little commercial center as it approaches Sulgrave. Ahead of it is the scenic backwoods climb up the Western Run valley. The photo was taken in June 1946.

R. S. Crockett

E. S. Miller

On April 24, 1949, the #25 line south of Kelly Avenue in Mt. Washington was switched to bus, leaving the rail line from Mt. Washington to Pimlico isolated from its downtown entry. This loop and bus transfer terminal was built at Kelly Avenue and Sulgrave as a temporary expedient until buses could be used over the full route, a service which began on September 14, 1950.

One reason for the two-step bus conversion of the Mt. Washington route was the private track and primitive state of the roads in the Western Run valley west of Mt. Washington. Semi-convertible No. 5583, working the Cheswolde shuttle, has just come down the valley and pauses at Kelly Avenue and Sulgrave in "downtown" Mt. Washington. At that time, Kelly Avenue was little more than a path alongside the tracks. When the car line was abandoned, the avenue was completely rebuilt. The scene is in May 1950.

Baltimore seemed to abound in rustic pockets within the city, and Kelly Avenue was one. Here No. 5583 eases downhill near Poplin Street, passing a tiny community built alongside Western Run. When the car line died, the community died too, for it was almost entirely obliterated by the widening and repaving project.

R. S. Crockett

[ABOVE:] **Arlington Junction, at the intersection of Kelly Avenue and Cross Country Boulevard, was the point where the Pimlico-Belvedere "main line" and the Cheswolde "jerkwater" branch divided. This May 1941 view looks west: on the left an inbound PCC from Belvedere loop and Pimlico glides by while the two-car enthusiast excursion has unloaded to watch the action. [RIGHT:] West of the junction, the Belvedere main line climbed curving Cross Country Boulevard toward Pimlico. This inbound Peter Witt is carefully descending at Chilham Road in May 1950.**

E. S. Miller

Onward to Pimlico. Peter Witt No. 6022 has finally surmounted the long, curving grades of Kelly Avenue and Cross Country Boulevard and rests at Cross Country and Ken Oak. This section was developed as Mt. Washington Heights in the early 1900s; the car line itself was opened in 1897.

Lucky streetcar riders could catch snatches of the races at Pimlico as cars followed Pimlico Road along the east side of the track, seen to the left in this May 1950 photo. Peter Witt No. 6021 is near Rogers Avenue on its way to Belvedere.

Both, E. S. Miller

E. S. Miller

[ABOVE:] **The Cheswolde branch looked much like a 1905-era rural trolley, but actually was built as a main line from Baltimore to Pikesville, Reisterstown and Glyndon. Built by the Baltimore & Northern in 1897, it followed Cross Country Boulevard and Greenspring Avenue west of Arlington Junction, then struck out across country to Pikesville. A redundant and trafficless line, it was cut back to a stub branch in 1923. This scene was typical: No. 5583 on Cross Country Boulevard at Greenspring Avenue, heading for Arlington Junction in 1950.** [RIGHT:] **Key Avenue was the early name of present Cheswolde Road, and for years after the name change, Cheswolde cars carried "Key Avenue" destination signs. No. 5394 rests on a well-trimmed front lawn at the "Key Avenue" and Greenspring terminal in March 1948. The track in front of the car once turned west for Pikesville.**

R. S. Crockett

51

NORTH SUBURBAN LINES

● **Guilford** ● **Roland Park** ● **Lakeside Park** ● **Towson** ●

The thriving collection of car lines in north Baltimore disappeared in the late 1940s as the major north-south arteries such as Calvert, St. Paul, Charles and Maryland Avenue were converted to one-way operation. It was a mixed blessing: the routes to Hampden, Roland Park and Guilford had varying amounts of private track and could move fast, but their routings below North Avenue tended to be tortuous.

G. J. Voith

Outbound #25 line PCC No. 7020, bound for Mt. Washington and Belvedere loop, is shown on Maryland Avenue at Lafayette in 1946. Poking out of Lafayette at the left is a #30 Fremont Avenue line car which has just made its terminal loop and will work its way west on North Avenue.

Typical of the convoluted downtown routings was that taken by this #29 Roland Park car, shown turning onto St. Paul Street from North Avenue by Polytechnic High School in 1947. To reach this point, it has traveled on Calvert Street, Read Street, Charles Street and North Avenue; it will proceed north on St. Paul to University Parkway where it will head west.

On the other hand, #1 Guilford-Gilmor line cars, such as this semi-convertible southbound on St. Paul at 21st Street, came out of town on Guilford Avenue (including a stretch on the elevated) to North Avenue, then headed west on North Avenue to St. Paul, north on St. Paul to 25th, then east again to Greenmount Avenue. But Baltimore was slower then, as this 1947 scene of the "placid rows" so strongly suggests.

Both, G. J. Voith

53

Skirting the north side of the Johns Hopkins University campus, an inbound PCC from Roland Park is rolling east on University Parkway near Charles Street. By this time car riders were buying shiny new autos such as the 1946 Buick whizzing past on the right or the more lowly Plymouth parked on the left.

Both, G. J. Voith

In 1916, a unique branch line was built to serve the newly developed and highly exclusive Guilford area. An extension of the St. Paul Street trackage, it followed gently curving upper St. Paul Street past wide lawns and large homes to Bedford Square at Charles Street. Its double track was split on the two sides of the roadway. Trimmed hedges separated the track and street, making the car line not only unobtrusive but almost invisible. Typical was this scene at St. Paul and 39th Street in 1947 as an inbound fan excursion poses.

End of the Guilford branch was at Bedford Square, where the divided tracks came together at an attractive waiting station. Here the camera looks southeast on St. Paul as No. 5591 arrives while another semi-convertible pulls away.

Bedford Square station itself, as it looked in March 1947. At this time the Guilford line was operated as a branch of the #1 Gilmor Street line, a roundabout line which looped through the center city and ended up at Druid Hill Park via Fulton Avenue. The shelter station still stands.

Both, R. S. Crockett

Roland Park was a pioneering planned upper class suburban community, first laid out in the early 1890s and landscaped by Frederick Law Olmsted. Part of the project was a "rapid transit" line downtown, following picturesque private track on Roland Avenue and University Parkway. [ABOVE:] Roland Park's commercial center was this aesthetic building at Roland Avenue and Upland. Built in 1896, it was the country's first integrated suburban shopping center—the great-grandfather of today's massive malls. The #29 line terminated here, and there was a carhouse directly to the rear. In this July 1946 scene, No. 5797 with a fan excursion has followed a regular #29 PCC into the terminal station. [RIGHT:] From the shopping center, car tracks continued north on Roland Avenue to its end at Lake Avenue, then dipped into the woods for a short but scenic run to Lakeside Park, a onetime picnic spot in a glen near Lake Roland. This lightly-populated upper Roland Avenue section was served by a separate line, #24, running from Lakeside to the Roland Park water tower at University Parkway. In June 1946, No. 5388 negotiates the rustic Lakeside Loop.

H. H. Harwood, Jr.

Baltimore's heaviest car line, the #8 route to Towson, followed York Road which, in the days before Interstate 83, was the primary motor route to York and much of central Pennsylvania. In the early days, this line had been a long country trolley ride to a sleepy county seat, passing large estates and summer homes along the way. But its charm diminished as the York Road corridor suburbanized and commercialized. A little of the country feeling remained on York Road south of Stevenson Lane on a late afternoon in October 1963 as southbound No. 7077 paused for a pickup. Within a month both the leaves and the car line would be gone.

[ABOVE:] **It obviously was a light morning on normally bustling York Road when inbound No. 7316 passed the old Sheppard Pratt Hospital entrance opposite Worcester Road in May 1951. Until 1930, the car tracks through this area were set in a private reservation on the east (right) side of the old two-lane turnpike.** [BELOW:] **Before 1958, Towson had both railroad and streetcar service. The two crossed at York Road and Susquehanna, shown here in May 1951 as Irvington-bound No. 7334 passed under the "Ma & Pa" bridge. A block to the left, the frame railroad station was still a stopping place for the leisurely passenger run to Delta and York. The stone bridge abutments continue to be York Road landmarks, although the frame house behind has been replaced by the main Baltimore County Public Library.**

Both, E. S. Miller

A. W. Maginnis

[TOP:] As MTA buses now do, Towson streetcars looped on Washington Avenue in front of the 1854 county court house. But the scene on the opposite side of Washington was much different when No. 7359 waited to start its long run to Catonsville in 1959. The block is now occupied almost wholly by new office buildings. [MIDDLE:] No. 7106 laid over on an evening in October 1963. [BOTTOM:] From the other side of the street, the court house dome pokes up between the leaves at the left. Between 1912 and 1923 the hapless battery-powered Towson & Cockeysville Electric Railway came into the square from the far left of this 1963 photo.

Both, H. H. Harwood, Jr.

NORTHEAST SUBURBAN LINES

● **Stadium** ● **Harford Road** ● **Belair Road** ●

R. S. Crockett

Baltimore had no major league sports teams in the 1940s, but crowds still came to the old Baltimore Stadium, Memorial Stadium's predecessor on the 33rd Street site. And many came by special streetcars, which reached the stadium over a spur running on Loch Raven Road from Gorsuch Avenue to 36th Street. Since the stadium branch had no regular service, the cars simply were stored in long lines along Loch Raven until the game ended.

60

G. J. Voith

[OPPOSITE PAGE:] **It's early summer in 1946 and the original minor league Orioles are playing, having been burned out of their own ball park on Greenmount Avenue in Waverly two years before.** [BOTTOM:] **And this lineup on Loch Raven is awaiting the end of the 1944 Army-Navy football game.** [BELOW:] **A more workaday northeast Baltimore trunk line was the #19 Harford Road route, which came out of downtown via Aisquith Street and Central Avenue. This outbound Parkville PCC is snaking through the "S" curve at the Central Avenue-Harford Road intersection in May 1950.**

E. S. Miller

The long, straight routes out Harford Road and Belair Road originally were semi-rural side-of-the-road lines serving small turnpike settlements. But rapid residential and commercial development along these arteries swallowed up the open fields, and street widening projects displaced the onetime private track. By the 1940s, both were rather ordinary streetcar lines noted more for traffic volume than scenery.

[ABOVE:] One pleasant exception was the section of the Harford Road route at Clifton Park, where a tree-lined right-of-way followed the east side of the road for close to a mile along the park border. Montpelier Street marked the south end of this scenic segment, shown here looking north in May 1951. [BELOW:] Four blocks farther north, PCC No. 7352 passes a small community commercial center at Abbottston Street, also in May 1951. Before 1947, cars of the wandering #17 line terminated here with a wye behind the cafe at the far right for turning the cars, then worked their way into town via Abbottston, Kirk Avenue, Gorsuch, Greenmount, 31st, and St. Paul—eventually winding up in Westport.

Both, E. S. Miller

[ABOVE:] **Southbound Peter Witt No. 6080 enters the private track at Erdman Avenue and Harford Road, at the north end of Clifton Park.** [BELOW:] **Another pretty interlude on Harford Road was the dip through the park in the Herring Run valley. Once called Hall's Springs after a still-active spring to the left of the photo, this was the terminal of a horse car line which struggled out Harford Road in the early 1870s. The onetime summer resort was much changed in 1952 as an inbound PCC dropped into the valley at Walther Avenue.**

Both, E. S. Miller

Harford Road cars ended their runs at Parkville loop, just north of Taylor Avenue. Between 1904 and 1936, a single-track rural "jerkwater" line extended beyond here to Carney, at Harford and Joppa Roads. The Carney trolley's diesel replacement has picked up five passengers from the #19 line PCC's at the left and soon will head north. The photo dates to April 1952; Harford Road trolleys ran until June 16, 1956.

Both, E. S. Miller

Wearing the short-lived yellow-green-light gray "fruit salad" colors of BTC's new owner, National City Lines, PCC No. 7038 heads into town on Belair Road at Sinclair Lane in July 1951. Behind is the B&O's Baltimore Belt Line, the main line to Philadelphia. A respectable passenger service still ran, but by then nothing stopped at the little wood shelter station behind the used car lot.

The east side of Clifton Park forms a pretty summer backdrop for yellow-orange Peter Witt No. 6032 running inbound on Belair Road near Cliftmont in July 1951.

Both, E. S. Miller

Belair Road's rolling topography added a little life to an otherwise bland trolley trip on the #15 line. Here an inbound PCC comes up out of the Herring Run valley at Pelham Avenue in mid-1951. Like the York Road and Harford Road routes, this line was originally laid on a roadside private right-of-way, but was relocated during street widening and repaving projects in 1928 and again in 1938. But at least it survived, for Belair Road was one of Baltimore's last two car lines.

EAST BALTIMORE LINES

● **Orangeville** ● **Highlandtown** ● **Canton** ● **Point Breeze** ●

East Baltimore once was crisscrossed with lines on such streets as Caroline, Preston, Federal, Orleans and Patterson Park Avenue, most of which were switched to bus or trackless trolley before World War II. One postwar survivor was the route out Monument Street to Kresson, in the Orangeville section of town, then a part of the #6 Curtis Bay line. Basically another "rowhouse line", its eastern extremity (built in stages between 1910 and 1917) was laid on a private way along the north side of Monument Street through a rather nondescript landscape.

G. J. Voith

Near the Kresson Street terminal, cars passed under two Pennsylvania Railroad bridges—in the foreground the branch to Canton, and in the rear, the high-speed main line to Philadelphia and New York, now Amtrak's Northeast Corridor route. Peter Witt No. 6036 is returning west in 1946; two-lane Monument Street is at the right.

G. J. Voith

E. S. Miller

[TOP:] **The Monument Street private track began here in the vicinity of Highland Avenue. Despite its "Monument & Kresson" sign, No. 6050 is westbound for Curtis Bay. The Baltimore Brick Company shed (now the site of a used car lot) was typical of this section's scenery.** [ABOVE:] **More charming were the streets in Canton, particularly when decorated by the old semi-convertibles. This #18 line car is at South Kenwood Avenue at Elliott Street in November 1949.**

[ABOVE:] **Cars of the #18 and #34 lines wound through the working community of Canton south of Eastern Avenue. Semi-convertible No. 5772, working the #18 Pennsylvania Avenue-Canton line, weaves its way on Essex Street at the Fait Street-Montford Avenue intersection in 1949.** [BELOW:] **A #34 "Third Street"-Canton car, No. 5727, changes ends at its stub terminal on Highland Avenue near Toone Street. This track once continued on south, eventually ending at Clinton Street and Holabird Avenue near the Canton waterfront.**

Both, E. S. Miller

E. S. Miller

[ABOVE:] **A semi-convertible on the #34 line glides down brick-paved Conkling Street on its way from Highlandtown into Canton. The view looks north at the Hudson Street intersection.** [BELOW:] **Another Canton-area route was the #20 Point Breeze, which served a more industrialized area along Oldham Street and Broening Highway. In earlier years it was famous as the line to Riverview Park at Colgate Creek; later it carried hordes of workers to the Western Electric plant on the old park site. En route, it worked its way through a maze of B&O and Pennsylvania Railroad industrial trackage, such as this crossing of the Pennsy's Dundalk-Sparrows Point branch at 16th Street. The car is an inbound fan excursion in September 1946.**

H. H. Harwood, Jr.

[LEFT:] A major landmark in Highlandtown, or "Hollandtown" in the local *patois,* is the elaborate series of underpasses carrying Eastern Avenue under Conrail's onetime Pennsylvania Railroad industrial branches to Canton and Fells Point. This 1947 view looks east as a two-car train of "red rockets" from Sparrows Point whines through the long dip. In the distance behind, a Pennsy steam switcher shuffles a cut of cars on the original Philadelphia, Wilmington & Baltimore Railway alignment. [BELOW:] Looking west from approximately the same spot toward Haven Street, the camera catches a pair of outbound "rockets".

Both, G. J. Voith

DUNDALK - SPARROWS POINT LINE

● Dundalk ● Turners Station ● Sparrows Point ●
● Bay Shore Park ● Fort Howard ●

Other East Baltimore lines were sideshows to the main event: the heavy, blue-collar Sparrows Point line serving the big Bethlehem Steel mill and shipyard complex at "The Point" and its bedroom communities of Dundalk and Turners Station. The mill was first developed in this remote southeastern corner of Baltimore's harbor in the late 1880s. In the mill's early days, workers either lived in the company town of Sparrows Point or rode to work on Pennsylvania Railroad local trains. The streetcar line across the flatlands and the wide Bear Creek estuary was completed in 1903; three years later it was extended beyond to Fort Howard and Bay Shore Park.

E. S. Miller

For much of its length beyond Highlandtown, the Sparrows Point route followed Dundalk Avenue and its extension, Main Street in Turners Station. It was a straight, fast, heavy-duty piece of railroad, equipped with the standard railroad fixtures of block signals and crossbucks. Here a single "red rocket" passes Fait Avenue north of Dundalk, now the site of the I-95 interchange, in May 1950.

[ABOVE:] "Test Drive the '50 Ford" says the car on the left, and many wartime trolley riders were buying. Also accompanying "red rocket" No. 5867 at Dundalk Avenue and Bayship are a classic Good Humor truck and an old bus made into a mobile lunchroom. The car is bound for Sparrows Point in July 1950. [BELOW:] The community of Dundalk was farmland before World War I, when Bethlehem Steel and the U. S. Shipping Board began development of a carefully planned suburb for the booming "Point". Dundalk was a pragmatic spot; its center was located at Center Place, whose center in turn was the trolley station. Single semi-convertible No. 5847 is loading for Highlandtown and downtown Baltimore in 1950.

Both, E. S. Miller

A Dundalk classic: Twin "rockets" from Sparrows Point roll along the straight, well-kept Dundalk Avenue speedway at Center Place in July 1950. This was close to their final hour. On July 29, 1950, the line between Highlandtown and downtown was cut, after which surplus PCC's took over most of the diminishing business.

All, E. S. Miller

South of Dundalk is Turners Station, shown in these two scenes along Main Street. The settlement was named for a point on the onetime Pennsylvania Railroad's Sparrows Point branch. Two fan excursions carry destination signs for Wolfe and Aliceanna Streets in Fells Point, which was never a terminal for Sparrows Point cars. [ABOVE:] No. 5787 is at Maryland Avenue and [RIGHT:] No. 5785 at the Riverside power plant in July 1950.

E. S. Miller

[ABOVE:] One of the more spectacular streetcar structures anywhere was the long trestle spanning Bear Creek, a wide bay estuary separating Sparrows Point from the "mainland". Highways into "The Point" dodged around to the north to cross where the creek was narrower; the car line struck straight across from Sollers Point. In August 1950, PCC's were strongly in evidence as a Sparrows Point semi-convertible meets its replacement at the Sollers Point end. [LEFT:] The swing span is open, probably for one of the many pleasure boats based in the various inlets in the area, in this April 1956 view from the front of a Sparrows Point PCC. The signal at the right was a variation of the "smashboard" design; not only was it an unmistakable stop signal, but should a car run through it, the blade would be broken and thus provide positive evidence that the motorman disobeyed the signal.

H. H. Harwood, Jr.

[RIGHT:] **On the Sparrows Point side, both the scenery and the atmosphere suddenly degenerated. Car riders were immediately plunged into Bethlehem Steel's sprawling mill and shipyard complex, one of the largest in the United States. A short distance beyond the trestle a branch swung south to a loop at the shipyard entrance. In this September 1953 view, the camera looks east on the main line into downtown Sparrows Point. The shipyard spur, opened in 1919, branches to the right.** [BELOW:] **Skirting steel mills and yards of the Patapsco & Back Rivers Railroad, Bethlehem's switching subsidiary, PCC No. 7057 is on its way to Sparrows Point terminal in April 1958, four months before service ended. The car is swinging onto a mill road which carried streetcar and motor traffic over the P&BR tracks on a steel viaduct.**

E. S. Miller

F. W. Schneider, III

Nestled in the midst of the mills was the town of Sparrows Point, the company-built community laid out in the days when the Point was remote from Baltimore and Dundalk did not exist. As company towns went, Sparrows Point was a model, well built and well kept. Cars came into the town from the north on 4th Street. Here southbound yellow-orange No. 5843 passes red No. 5836 on the northern outskirts in 1950.

Both, E. S. Miller

In November 1950, semi-convertible No. 5857 trundled down D Street in the town of Sparrows Point as track and paving work was under way. In Sparrows Point's stratified society, D Street houses were reserved for middle and lower level managers. Now the town is gone. What one newspaper once called "the cleanest and greenest steel mill town in the USA" was bulldozed for mill expansion in 1973.

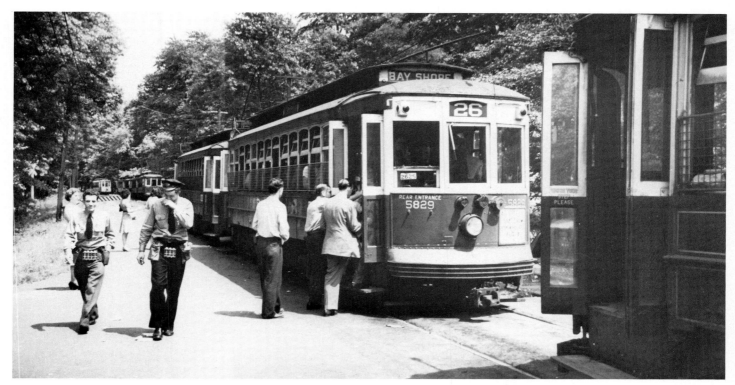

G. J. Voith

Sparrows Point terminal, at the east end of town, was a busy spot, especially in the summer when crowds heading for Bay Shore Park transferred here to the shuttles running east to the park on Chesapeake Bay. Shuttles also connected here for Fort Howard. This view looks east in 1945. In the distance is the right-of-way to Bay Shore and Fort Howard. One of the two tracks usually was used for car storage.

The scene was a good bit more barren by 1956. Once a wooded haven beyond the mills, the Sparrows Point terminal looked like this in its later days. In 1950, a loop had been built for the PCC's. The Bay Shore branch died after the 1946 summer season and Fort Howard service ended in 1953. Afterwards, mill expansion swallowed up the old right-of-way, seen directly behind the car.

H. H. Harwood, Jr.

Built in 1906, the Bay Shore-Fort Howard extension seemed to be constantly hopping creeks. Originally built in a big loop circling the peninsula along Chesapeake Bay, the line was cut into two stub end branches when a hurricane removed the trestle over Shallow Creek in the loop's center in 1933. This trestle carried the two lines over Jones Creek, a short distance east of Sparrows Point. A Fort Howard shuttle car crosses in October 1946.

R. S. Crockett

G. J. Voith

A onetime UR&E trolley park—and one of Baltimore's most popular—Bay Shore opened in 1906. Soon after, crowds came in by the trainloads for swimming in the bay, picnicking and riding the park rides which eventually included a roller coaster. At the end of the line in 1945, semi-convertible No. 5842 waits to return to Sparrows Point.

G. V. Arnoux

Cars loaded under this large shed next to the roller coaster in the park center. Bethlehem Steel bought the park property in 1947 and demolished its buildings, but as yet has not used the site. Oddly, however, the streetcar terminal shed still stood in 1983.

Considerably less exciting was the other stub terminal at Fort Howard, seen in October 1946.

R. S. Crockett

SOUTH SUBURBAN LINES

● **Fort McHenry** ● **Westport** ● **Brooklyn** ● **Fairfield** ● **Curtis Bay** ●

The areas south of downtown Baltimore were, and still are, working communities oriented to the docks and industries which developed around the south side of the harbor: shipbuilding, chemicals, petroleum, scrap and sugar refining. Thus the streetcar lines serving them were unglamorous, but offered a lot of vitality and interest.

G. J. Voith

The #2 Fort Avenue line crossed Baltimore's other "point"—Locust Point, a beehive of B&O and Western Maryland piers, drydocks, and port-related industry. But it also ended at Baltimore's premier tourist attraction, Fort McHenry. Here No. 5201 poses at the Fort gate on a 1947 fantrip. Regular cars ended their runs on a loop at the right.

[ABOVE:] **Passengers inside PCC No. 7108 brace themselves for the jolts as the inbound Westport car crosses the B&O's four-track main line at Ridgely Street in 1946. In the days before the Russell Street bridge, traffic often jammed up at this active crossing waiting for the parades of passenger trains, freights, light engines and Baltimore & Annapolis interurban trains. Between 1935 and 1950, the B&A used these tracks from Camden Station to its own line in Westport.** [BELOW:] **Inbound semi-convertible No. 5648 picks up a hitchhiker on Annapolis Road in Westport. Just ahead is the Western Maryland Railway crossing, followed closely by the B&O's Curtis Bay branch crossing.**

Both, G. J. Voith

G. J. Voith

Nearing its terminal at Waterview Avenue, No. 7110 rolls up the hill on Annapolis Road in 1947. Streetcars first came to Westport in 1896. By the early 1900s, the little community on the Patapsco's Middle Branch also had two steam railroads (the B&O and Western Maryland) and two electric interurban lines—the Washington, Baltimore & Annapolis and the Annapolis Short Line.

Westport still had two electric lines when this photo was taken in 1947. Emerging from the onetime WB&A's Westport tunnel is Baltimore & Annapolis No. 205, bound for Annapolis over a section of the original double-track WB&A main line opened in 1908. Directly above, a BTC PCC car lays over at the Westport loop at Annapolis Road and Waterview Avenue. This scene has been obliterated by the Baltimore-Washington Parkway, which occupies the area immediately to the right of the tunnel. Oddly, however, the tunnel remains intact, although well disguised.

R. S. Crockett

G. J. Voith

Gateway to Brooklyn and Curtis Bay was the impressive 1917 Hanover Street bridge, which in the mid-1940s carried a constant parade of #6 streetcars to and from the heavy industries and the coal pier at Curtis Bay and Fairfield. Peter Witt No. 6074 is on its way south in 1947.

R. S. Crockett

Mainstays of the Curtis Bay-Fairfield line, the austere-looking Peter Witts seemed to fit their bleak surroundings. This one is returning downtown from the Fairfield branch, a large loop serving the shipyards and refineries on the East Brooklyn-Fairfield peninsula. The camera looks east from the B&O overpass at Patapsco Avenue and Shell Road on the last day of service, March 20, 1948.

G. J. Voith

A short distance away, inbound Peter Witt No. 6051 comes around the west side of the Fairfield loop in 1947. This branch was a World War I project, opened in 1918. In 1941 the original loop was extended to the northeast to reach closer to the wartime Bethlehem Steel shipyard (now gone) and the Maryland Drydock facilities.

[ABOVE:] **If anything, the line into Curtis Bay was grimmer than the Fairfield branch, as this view along Curtis Avenue attests.** [BELOW:] **Curtis Bay loop terminal was in this no-man's land south of Aspen Street and Curtis Avenue, seen just as service was ending.**

WORK EQUIPMENT

Like those of most streetcar systems, Baltimore Transit's work equipment was a melange of hand-me-downs, rebuilds, and utilitarian built-for-the-purpose cars. [LEFT:] Test car No. 3550, used for rail bond testing, fell into the hand-me-down category. A 1904 Brill product, it obviously started life as a passenger car. Here it suns itself at Govans loop on November 2, 1963, the last day of service. It subsequently was saved by the Baltimore Streetcar Museum. [BELOW:] A genuine high wire act: line car No. 3503 and its nerveless crew work on the Guilford "el" overhead. By the time this July 1947 photo was taken, BTC was using motor trucks for most of its wire maintenance, but private rights-of-way and locations such as this obviously required a rail car.

H. H. Harwood, Jr.

R. W. Janssen

Snow brought out the sweepers, such as No. 3239 shown whirling its way east on North Avenue at Maryland Avenue during a heavy (for Baltimore) fall in December 1948.

During the same snowfall, sweeper No. 3217 swung its wing plow into position to clear the sloppiness at the right side of the rails on Maryland Avenue.

Crane No. 3736 blocks a line of trackless trolleys at Howard and Lombard Streets in October 1947 as it removes rail from a crossing abandoned over seven years earlier.

All, R. W. Janssen

SURVIVORS

As THIS IS WRITTEN in 1984, it has been 21 years since Baltimore's last streetcar ran. Many lines have been gone 30 years or more. Their tracks long since have been covered with asphalt or removed completely. What was once grassy open private track has been made into new streets, swallowed up by street widenings, or simply left to revert to nature. Occasionally you can spot bits of rail tentatively poking up through the pavement, or perhaps make out telltale ridges running down the center of some street marking some thinly-buried car line. But these aren't much more than fleeting reminders, for the next street surfacing project will submerge them again or finally extract them.

In some sections of the city, the entire environment in which the streetcars operated has been obliterated. Indeed, it is impossible to relate trolleys to, say, the present Inner Harbor or to the Charles Center-Civic Center-Convention Center complexes. It is equally difficult to picture the Harford Road exit of the Beltway as a two-lane rural road with the single track of the Carney "jerkwater" running alongside it. Seemingly the city's streetcar system has vanished completely and irrevocably.

Well, not entirely. The tracks themselves, although many still lurk under the street surface, may not be visible. But quite a few of the structures which served the cars and sheltered their passengers can be seen today—if you know where to look. In fact, Baltimore has what is probably the richest and most comprehensive collection of old street railway buildings anywhere. Still standing, and mostly in healthy condition, are three ornate stations of a Civil War-era steam dummy line, a horse car terminal, four cable railway powerhouses, a large turn-of-the-century shop and powerhouse, and a miscellaneous assortment of carhouses and terminal buildings. In short, chapters from the entire history of the street railway in Baltimore still exist in brick, stone and concrete.

The mandatory starting point for any streetcar archeologist is at the southern end of Druid Hill Park. Here in the space of only a few blocks are relics representing the oldest, newest, and almost every phase in between. Almost from its earliest days, the park was a focus for car lines, and important terminal structures were regularly built there and then discarded for something newer. Happily, the area was bypassed by later develop-

ment and also somehow escaped urban renewal, thus allowing much to remain amazingly intact.

Let's start with the oldest. On the northwest corner of Druid Hill and Fulton Avenues is a gingerbready open pavilion looking forlorn and lost alongside this hectic intersection. Probably built in the mid-1860s, it originally served as a station on the City Park Railway, a horse car and later steam dummy line built in 1863 to connect the park with North Avenue. As built, the little station was an exuberant Victorian-Oriental confection with a pagoda-like roof once called the "Chinese station". The Park Railway was dismantled in 1879 but the station-pavilion continued in use, successively serving city horse cars, cable cars, electric trolleys, and now buses. Its roof ornamentation long since has been stripped and subdued and the structure itself somewhat reduced in size, but much is still original.

Elsewhere in Druid Hill Park are two other one-time Park Railway stations, both of them even more fanciful. The large Council Grove pavilion opposite the Zoo entrance was the line's northern terminal. After years of neglect and a close brush with destruction, it was restored in 1972 and now looks precisely as it did when the little steam cars loaded there. The "dummy line" also had a way station at what is now Auchentoroly Terrace and Orem Avenue. Smaller than the others but equally exotic, this Oriental-eclectic structure subsequently was picked up and moved to the hillside overlooking Druid Lake where it lives on as the Latrobe pavilion.

Not far away, a more workaday relic of the horse car era stands on the east side of Druid Hill Avenue at Retreat Street. This picturesque stone and brick building dates to 1885 and was built as the carhouse and general office of the Peoples Railway Company, one of several early companies which competed for park traffic. Perhaps appropriately, it is now an auto garage, but the name of its original owner still can be seen carved in stone over its central entrance.

Coincidentally, the ponderously ornate hulk diagonally across the street at the southwest corner of Druid Hill and Retreat is the country's finest survivor of the short-lived cable railway era. Built by the Baltimore Traction Company in 1890-1891, the massive structure was a combination carhouse and powerhouse. Inside its north end, two Corliss stationary steam engines operated the under-street

**Originally equipped with a soaring pagoda-style roof with ornate wood embellish-
ments, the Fulton waiting station looked like this in 1983. It has served every form of
Baltimore transit vehicle—horse cars, cable cars, trolleys, trackless trolleys and
buses.**

cables which moved the cars on the northern half
of Baltimore Traction's Druid Hill-Patterson Park
route. After abandonment of the cable system in
1896, the building briefly was used as an electric
carhouse. Now, with most of its windows and doors
bricked up, it's a warehouse. But there's no question
about its heritage—the name "Baltimore Traction"
clearly stands out in stone over the warehouse doors.

Less than two blocks to the east was once
Baltimore's most elegant late Victorian carhouse.
It's there still, but only a semblance of what it once
was. The present single-story warehouse in the
block bounded by Madison Avenue, Cloverdale and
McCulloh Streets was originally the carhouse and
general office of the Baltimore City Passenger Railway—still another of the fiercely independent
companies in the days before the "United". Its
northeast corner originally incorporated a three-story

office building alive with spires, gables and or-
namental ironwork. The carhouse was sold in 1947
and the two top stories were cut down soon after.
A few original iron filigrees still hang on from the
glory days.

The final stop on our Druid Hill historical tour
is back where we started at Druid Hill and Fulton
Avenues. Directly across the street from the old steam
dummy station is its architectural opposite—the
huge fortresslike former Park Terminal. Built in 1909
to replace the mishmash of obsolete carhouses in the
area, Park Terminal was the model of a modern,
efficient streetcar storage and servicing facility. It
also originally housed company offices. Closed in
1952 and now owned by the city, it has been
remodeled slightly but is esentially unchanged. Look
above its two main entrance doors and you'll see
"Park Terminal" carved in stone over one and "Waiting

[TOP:] **The Victorian-Moorish Latrobe pavilion, once a City Park Railway way station near Auchentoroly Terrace and Orem Avenue, was relocated to the east side of Druid Lake where it still stands.** [MIDDLE:] **Terminal of the long-abandoned steam dummy line was the Council Grove pavilion at the present Zoo entrance, seen here in 1981. The scrollsaw woodwork on the roof was made new when the structure was restored, but it follows the lines of the original, removed many years ago.** [BOTTOM:] **Quite elegant by horse car terminal standards, the onetime Peoples Railway carhouse and office was built in 1885. Note the words "Peoples....Co." over the front door; the "Railway" part has been covered by the modern sign mount.**

All, H. H. Harwood, Jr.

The gloomy Romanesque Druid Hill Avenue cable powerhouse and carhouse dates to 1891. The view faces north on Druid Hill Avenue toward Retreat Street. The section nearest the camera was the carhouse. The adjoining portion housed the stationary steam engines which propelled the under-street cables.

Room" over the other. Immediately south of Park Terminal is the brick 1890s-era terminal of the Central Railway, which was later used as a substation building.

Other bits of street railway history can be found in all corners of the city. Three other cable powerhouses survive—more, in fact, than anywhere else in the country. Two of them are close neighbors in East Baltimore—one on the north side of Pratt Street west of Central Avenue (built by Baltimore Traction in 1890-91) and the other on the north side of East Baltimore Street at Aisquith dating to 1892-93. The cable system turned out to be an expensive mistake and the lines were electrified in the late 1890s; neither building served its original purpose more than five years. The Pratt Street structure is now a city-owned garage; the East Baltimore Street building has had a variety of uses, recently as an ice cream plant. The third surviving powerhouse is harder to spot but probably more familiar. Located on the east side of Charles Street north of Lanvale, the onetime Baltimore City Passenger Railway powerhouse-carhouse complex is now the Charles Theater and the Famous Ballroom.

When Baltimore's gaggle of independent streetcar companies was consolidated into the United Railways & Electric Company in 1899, one of the UR&E's first major projects was a single centralized shop to handle all heavy repairs and car rebuildings for the system. It picked a vast piece of property on Washington Boulevard opposite Carroll Park and started from scratch with a first-class facility. E. Francis Baldwin, a creative and certainly versatile Baltimore architect, was hired to design it. Baldwin had produced an incredible variety of commercial, ecclesiastical and industrial buildings in the city and elsewhere—including such past and present landmarks as the Mt. Royal Station, Maryland Club, Fidelity building, Old City College, the present B&O Museum roundhouse and the now-departed Rennert Hotel and St. Marys Seminary. He also had built a string of very attractive stations along the B&O system. Carroll Park shop was completed in 1901 and consisted of two immense monitor-roofed buildings incorporating four bays each, plus extensive outside storage trackage. Baldwin built well at Carroll Park; the shop survived the transition from streetcar to bus and is still the operating and

All, *H. H. Harwood, Jr.*

Park Terminal, as seen from the Druid Hill avenue side in 1983. The passenger waiting station was at the northeast corner, seen at the far right in this photograph. UR&E division operating offices originally were on the second floor.

Baltimore City Passenger Railway's short-lived 1893 East Baltimore Street cable powerhouse served most of its life as a Hendler creamery and ice cream plant. It is now a warehouse.

Its close neighbor, the 1891 Baltimore Traction East Pratt Street powerhouse is a contrast in architectural style and state of preservation. The view looks north from Central Avenue in 1975.

maintenance heart of the MTA bus system, the "United's" lineal descendent.

The UR&E also spotted new carhouses strategically around the city to supplement and replace the motley assortment of structures inherited from its predecessors. Similar in style to Park Terminal, they were solid, stolid structures built of brick and concrete; complete with parapets and battlements, they looked like they could withstand anything. And withstand they did. All but one were closed as the trolleys were phased out, but most were saved by their efficient design and low-maintenance construction. Still standing in 1984 (in addition to Park Terminal) were carhouses on Edmondson Avenue at Poplar Grove, York Road near Northway, North Avenue west of Gay Street and Lombard Street at Haven in Highlandtown. All were built in the 1907-08 period. Incidentally, most if not all of these also came off the drawing board of Francis Baldwin. Surviving in altered form as an MTA bus garage

is the 1913 Montebello carhouse on Harford Road, the United's newest large carhouse. Several other older carhouses also serve varying uses—one on West 25th Street at Howard, now an auto dealer, and one on West Baltimore Street at Smallwood. Another is located at Preston and Potomac Streets and a one-time horse car stable stands on Thames Street in Fells Point.

Although it's usually not thought of as a street railway structure, the hulking Pier 4 powerhouse in the Inner Harbor complex was another United Railways & Electric project. Originally built to centralize streetcar power generation, the big coal-fired plant was first started about 1900 but completed in at least three different sections at varying times later. It was situated to receive coal from barges via an elaborate conveyor system, since removed, and was also reached by railroad sidings from the B&O's Pratt Street track. Idle for many years, the old plant has been alternatively threatened with

H. H. Harwood, Jr.

Recycled several times over, the Charles Theater dates to 1893 and housed steam engines for Baltimore City Passenger Railway's north side cable route which ran to 25th and St. Paul via Calvert, Charles and St. Paul Streets. It first became a theater in 1939. To the left is the well-altered cable carhouse, later a bus garage and now the Famous Ballroom.

York Road carhouse, then and now. Typical of the "modern" 1907 and 1908 UR&E carhouses, the big York Road structure was one of the last two active survivors. Seen in the top view in October 1963 just before the end of service, it had become a lumber and hardware store by 1984. Customers enter through a side door around the far corner. Besides the obvious sealing of doors and windows, the ornate but useless parapets have been removed.

demolition and studied for some sort of adaptive use. After several false starts, it apparently now has a secure future as an indoor amusement park.

Also scattered around the city are several small streetcar waiting stations such as the attractive little structure at Bedford Square (Charles and St. Paul Streets). Still in fine condition, this one was built about 1916 as the terminal of the Guilford car line; later, as Homeland was built up to the north, it also served as the transfer point for a feeder bus line. Somewhat lesser trolley stations stand at Overlea, University Parkway east of Roland Avenue, and Catonsville Junction (Edmondson Avenue east of

Dutton). And in Mt. Washington, a relatively elaborate 1897 trolley station survives at the northeast corner of Kelly Avenue and Sulgrave. Extensively altered, it is now an animal hospital.

Beside its city streetcar system, Baltimore also had one of the country's finest high-speed electric interurban lines—the Washington, Baltimore & Annapolis. The WB&A died of financial malnutrition in 1935, although its Baltimore-Annapolis segment carried passengers until 1950 under the auspices of the Baltimore & Annapolis Railroad. Despite its durable construction and elaborate engineering, the WB&A left only two relics in Baltimore, both of them now so well disguised that only the hardest-core railroad historian recognizes them. Yet both are common sights on well-beaten paths.

First is the line's original 1908 Baltimore terminal and general office building, a brick structure which sits in the center of the triangular block bounded by Liberty Street, Park Avenue and Lexington. Currently it is an Equitable Bank branch and gives little clue that it once incorporated an open trainshed on its ground floor. The WB&A vacated the building in 1921 when it moved to a much larger terminal taking up most of the block of Howard-Lombard-Eutaw-Pratt Streets; ironically the old station far outlived the new, which was demolished for the Downtown Holiday Inn.

Much more esoteric is the WB&A's Westport tunnel, which took the double-track electric line through the hill in the area of Annapolis Road and Waterview Avenue. Although really a rather garden-variety concrete subway structure, it was an early example (1907-1908) and had the distinction of being one of the very few interurban tunnels in the United States. Baltimore & Annapolis trains used it until February 1950; afterwards the Baltimore-Washington Parkway was built on this section of the old roadbed. But for some reason the interurban tunnel was bypassed and not touched. Still intact, albeit sealed and re-faced with stone, it can be seen alongside the west side of the Parkway just north of the Annapolis Road exit.

And finally, don't overlook the obvious: the Baltimore Streetcar Museum. Like the structures just mentioned, the BSM's collection covers the full span of Baltimore's transit history, from horse cars to one of the last PCC streamliners. But unlike the onetime shops and carhouses, this slice of history isn't static. Part of the collection operates regularly and—money, manpower and natural disasters permitting—all will do so some day. It is a genuinely unique collection—the only one covering a single city's public transportation from end to end; its existence is an amazing combination of foresight (by the old UR&E, which assembled most of it), perserverance (by BSM members, through one near-fatal false start and one flood), and spots of good fortune (with City help). Baltimore's streetcar era was a part of its past life and no past life really can be brought back. But happily the mementoes are alive.

There were period costumes and lots of smiles on July 11, 1954, when the fine vintage streetcar collection originally preserved by the UR&E was formally transferred to the Maryland Historical Society for custody until an operating museum could be established. The smiles turned out to be premature; it would be 16 years before any of the cars would operate at the Baltimore Streetcar Museum site on Falls Road. In the meantime, the collection came close to being lost after an abortive attempt to set up the museum in Robert E. Lee Park at Lake Roland. This happy scene is at Irvington loop, close to the Irvington carhouse where the collection had been stored for many years. The little No. 4732 was first built as a horse car about 1888 and was converted to an electric trolley in 1896.

T. F. Gleichmann, Jr.

H. H. Harwood, Jr.

Today at the Baltimore Streetcar Museum: Two samples of turn-of-the-century streetcar technology are exercised at the BSM terminal on Falls Road near North Avenue. At the left, No. 3828, a 1902 Brill product waits at the loop by the visitor's center. In the center, partially restored No. 3651 built by Brownell Car Company in 1898 is moved into the carhouse. The B&O's Baltimore Belt Line bridge provides regular views of present day railroading.

[OPPOSITE:] Probably the single most memorable Baltimore streetcar ride was the trip "out to sea" over the Bear Creek trestle to Sparrows Point. Forget the mills in the murk behind—Bay Shore Park and a swim in Chesapeake Bay was beyond through the woods at the end of the line. — *E. S. Miller.*